GW00367424

CONTENTS

A CONVICT HERITAGE

The colonies of Australia were used as penal settlements for about 162 000 men, women and children transported from Britain between 1788 and 1868.

It was these people who cultivated the first paddocks and gathered the first harvests. On the earliest journeys into the unknown interior of the continent, it was convicts who acted as carriers for the explorers. And when the Blue Mountains had been crossed, the convicts built the first roads, even though they were bound with chains and confined at night in boxes so small that they could not lie down to sleep.

In many places, time has removed the results of their labours. The buildings they erected in the short-lived northern settlements at Melville Island in 1824 and Port Essington in 1844-45 were soon overrun by tropical scrub after these outposts were abandoned.

Similarly, there are few traces of convicts in Melbourne, where some were housed in hulks; and none in South Australia, which was inhabited only by free settlers.

The most obvious remains are the later work of transported prisoners such as Fremantle Gaol in Western Australia which was built in 1856.

St Matthew's Church,
Windsor

Many examples of convict buildings can be seen in Tasmania. As well as the ruins of the notorious "model prison" at Port Arthur, other convict buildings include Constitution Dock in Hobart, and the oldest surviving bridge in Australia — the one across the Coal River — built at Richmond in 1823.

In Brisbane, the Observatory on Wickham Terrace (originally a windmill) has long been a prominent landmark and is one of two surviving convict buildings. The other is the Commissariat between William Street and Queen's Wharf Road.

Only at Norfolk Island far into the Pacific Ocean do the remains of buildings from the second period of convict habitation (1826-56) give a picture of what a penal settlement might have looked like when it was in use.

But it is in New South Wales, particularly in Sydney and its outer suburbs, where many of the best-preserved convict buildings can still be seen. The famous churches of St James in Sydney and St Matthew's at Windsor were designed by Francis Greenway, a convict architect, and built by convict labour. Others include such National Trust gems as Vaucluse House overlooking the harbour and Experiment Farm Cottage at Parramatta.

WHO WERE THE CONVICTS?

From 1788 to about 1825, the majority of men and women sentenced to transportation were thieves. Afterwards, more violent criminals were sent. It was a time of over-population and under-employment in England and some of these people had to steal if they wished to survive. But for many, crime had become their business. One boy of 11 boasted that he had been a thief since he was seven years old.

Officially, all male convicts had to be healthy, less than 50 years old and sentenced to "life" or 14 years. But older men, sick ones, and some on seven-year sentences were also used to fill up the ships going to Australia.

Mary Reibey

Simeon Lord

Although most of the convicts were from England, Ireland and Scotland, others included negroes, men from British colonies in India and even a Ukrainian. Later, 140 rebels were exiled from Canada to Australia.

Throughout the period of transportation, there was a very small number of educated men. These few could read and write, and because of this their stories have been given the most publicity. Many were forgers but others were pick-pockets, abductors or guilty of fraud. Some later reached important positions in the colony. They became traders like Simeon Lord and Mary Reibey; painters like Thomas Watling, Joseph Lycett and John Eyre; or writers including James

Hardy Vaux and James Tucker, author of the classic early account of convict life *Ralph Rashleigh*.

There were about 400 men from the British navy and army who had deserted, taken part in mutinies, or in some other way had disobeyed the strict regulations of those times.

Finally, there were the political prisoners, probably no more than 1000, whose ideas were too far ahead of their time. The five Scottish martyrs sent out in 1794, and the 60 Chartists in 1842, wanted votes for everybody in political elections.

The Luddites were some of the men who lost their jobs in factories when machinery was introduced. After protesting because they could no longer earn a living, about 200 were transported between 1813 and 1816. Similarly, the six Tolpuddle Martyrs were farm labourers who wanted to form a trade union. They hoped to persuade wealthy landowners to pay them more than a starvation wage.

The Irish were different. Overall, they made up about one third of all people transported to Australia. Most were transported not because they were criminals but because they were vagrants with nowhere to live. There were also a few rebels and political agitators.

Convicts boarding the prison hulk at Portsmouth in which the Tolpuddle Martyrs were confined while awaiting transportation

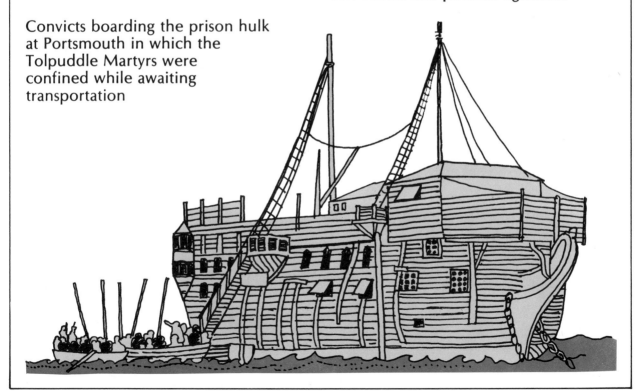

AN EARLY SUCCESS STORY

During the first four years of settlement at Sydney Cove and Parramatta, life was hard for everyone. Few convicts were given any housing. Joseph Smith arrived when he was 14 with a seven-year sentence. At first he lived for 17 weeks in a burnt-out hollow tree with 18 other convicts.

They wore rags because clothes could not be replaced until new supplies arrived from England. Their one cooking utensil was a "kettle", a large iron pot with a wooden bottom. "We used to stick it into a hole in the ground and make a fire around it," he wrote. When rations were shortest, they killed a dingo, pounded up some grass and cooked them together into soup.

Often he was yoked like a bullock with 20 or 30 other convicts to drag huge logs to the saw-pits.

Yet Smith was a success. When his sentence expired, he stowed away on a boat to Norfolk Island where he became overseer-gardener for Philip Gidley King, the Lieutenant-Governor. Smith also worked for D'Arcy Wentworth and later became a cedar cutter on the Hawkesbury. Eventually he married, saved his wages and bought a 16 hectare farm. In 1845, when he was about 70, he owned three other farms, 500 cattle and another 32 hectares of land surrounding his home. He also had £1000 in the bank.

Was Joseph Smith an exception, or were there many other success stories like his? This is something that the records rarely reveal. Possibly it is because so many of the people transported to Australia could neither read nor write.

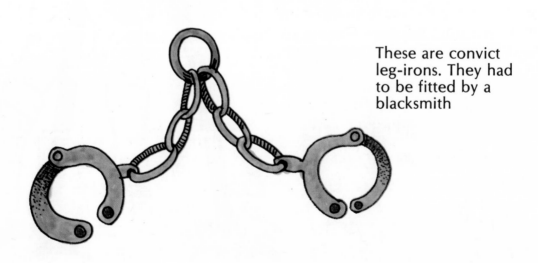

These are convict leg-irons. They had to be fitted by a blacksmith

THE LASH

For most of the period that convicts were transported to Australia, the most common punishment was a flogging. This was administered with a "cat-o'-nine tails" — a short-handled whip with nine leather lashes, each knotted at the end round a piece of metal.

Because flogging must be mentioned repeatedly in these pages, one way to show how harsh this punishment was is to print some first-hand descriptions.

In 1804, there was a revolt of Irish convicts at Castle Hill outside Sydney. Some of the ringleaders were hanged without trial. Others were sentenced to floggings of 300 lashes. These were described by Joseph Holt, a former rebel leader, who did not take part in the rising: "The unfortunate had his arms stretched round a tree, his two wrists tied with cords, and his breast pressed closely to the tree, so that flinching from the blow was out of the question, as it was impossible for him to stir...two men were appointed to flog. They stood on each side of Fitzgerald; and I never saw two threshers in a barn move their flails with more regularity than these two man-killers did, unmoved by pity, and rather enjoying their horrid employment..."

"The very first blows made the blood spout from Fitzgerald's shoulders...The day was windy, and I protest that although I was at least 15 yards to leeward from the sufferers, the blood, skin and flesh blew in my face as the executioners shook it off the cats. Fitzgerald received his whole 300 lashes during which Dr Mason used to go up to him occasionally and feel his pulse, it being contrary to law to flog a man beyond 50 lashes without having a doctor present. I shall never forget this humane doctor as he smiled and said, 'Go on; this man will tire you both before he fails...'"

The next prisoner was a lad about 20 years old, who also received 300 lashes. "The first hundred were given on his shoulders, and he was cut to the bone between the shoulder blades, which were both bare. The doctor then directed the next hundred to be inflicted lower down, which reduced his flesh to such a jelly that the doctor ordered him to have the remaining hundred on the calves of his legs. During the whole time, Galvin never even whimpered or flinched, if, indeed, it had been possible for him to have done so."

A cat-o'-nine tails

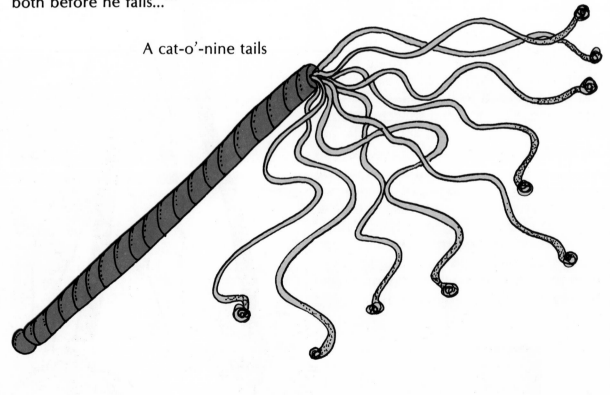

It is a wonder that those men could have remained alive. At Norfolk Island, where 1000 lashes could be given, a prisoner might receive 300, then be put into hospital to recover. He was then taken back to the triangle (the frame to which prisoners were sometimes tied) to receive the remainder of his sentence in one or two more floggings.

A final comment on what was a much less harsh punishment comes from the Superintendent of Hyde Park Barracks, Sydney, in September 1833. Among others he listed: "Daniel Dickson (for) disobeying orders, 50 lashes. The man was never flogged before; he cried out loudly at every lash; the skin was lacerated at the 17th lash. Twenty-five lashes would have been sufficient punishment; he fainted at the 30th lash; he was severely punished."

THE WOMEN CONVICTS

When transportation was planned, the British Government knew that it was not good enough to send just men. Officers and marines would need servants; convicts who had served their sentences would want wives. The government even suggested to Phillip that he call at Tonga and obtain Polynesian women to equalize the numbers as there was only one woman to every three male convicts sent on the First Fleet. But this did not happen.

The women sent to Australia were all supposed to be less than 45 years old and healthy. The average age was 24 but one woman in the First Fleet was 82 years old. Some had bribed gaolers to let them sail with their convicted lovers; others formed attachments on the voyage. As early as 10 February 1788, Reverend

The Female Factory, Parramatta

Richard Johnson married 14 couples. When others decided to marry, they were given a ticket-of-leave (freedom to work and live in a particular district provided they reported regularly to the authorities) or a conditional pardon which allowed them freedom to go anywhere within the colony. But as the colony grew older, the differences in numbers between men and women grew larger. By 1820, there was only one woman for every 15 men in the colony.

Like the men, the women were also a mixed lot. A few, like Elizabeth Perry who married James Ruse, attracted no attention. Phillip described her behaviour as "exemplary". Others were employed by officers, marines, soldiers and convict overseers and later became their unmarried wives.

The remainder were a problem. They were mothers of illegitimate children, or women who would not work as servants or gardeners. Until the first female factory was built at Parramatta in 1804, some women were forced to live with men just to get food and shelter; others lived together in huts made from wooden slabs and with bark roofs.

The work of women who were not assigned to permanent jobs as servants was to "pick oakum" (pull apart tarred rope ends which would then be used to seal cracks in ships' timbers), spin and weave wool and hemp, and make up "slops" (clothing) for the men.

Those who lived in the factory were rebellious as many were hardened criminals. Even later when Macquarie made Greenway design and build a £6000 three-storey brick building to house them, the problem was not solved. Although they were supposed to "maintain order, cleanliness, perfect obedience and *silence*", and were allowed to earn money from their needlework, most of these women were beyond reform. They were often drunk and could not be properly disciplined. Some were occasionally punished by having their heads shaved; others were made to wear heavy iron bands around their necks.

THE FIRST BUSHRANGER

The name "bushranger" came from those convicts, often twice convicted, who escaped from penal settlements and ranged free in the bush. They stole what they needed and sometimes killed those who tried to stop them. They first formed into gangs in Van Diemen's Land (Tasmania) about 1812.

The first bushranger was John "Black" Caesar, a Madagascar-born negro who arrived with the First Fleet. Little is known of his background or how he reached England. In 1785 he received the light sentence of seven years' transportation. Caesar was more than 183cm (6 feet) tall and was described as the hardest-working convict in the colony. He was as strong as an ox.

He was not really a troublemaker but his size gave him a large appetite. When Phillip first gave everyone the same rations, Caesar could not get enough to eat and was always hungry. When the rations were cut to a third, Caesar either had to steal or starve, although stealing food could be punished by hanging.

In April 1789, when he was caught stealing with "Black Jemmey", another negro, Jemmey was given 500 lashes. Caesar's sentence was increased to "life", but he just laughed. Two weeks later he stole a marine's musket and "went bush".

Judge Advocate David Collins said that for the next seven years, Caesar gave more trouble than any other convict in the settlement.

Once he was loaded with leg irons and made to dig a vegetable plot on Garden Island, now the RAN base in Sydney. After his irons were removed for good behaviour, he waited a week or two, then stole another gun and went bush again. He tried to join the local Aborigines but they would not have him.

He was sent to Norfolk Island for four years but when he returned to Sydney, he had not improved. He was just as hungry, still good humoured, and seemed to think that escaping was a sport. During the next year or so, he alternated between roaming free in the bush, or being caught and punished.

In January 1796, Caesar was again free but this time other men had escaped and the Acting-Governor, Major Francis Grose, feared that they might form into a gang. He offered what was then a huge reward — "five gallons (about 23 litres) of rum" for Caesar's capture. In February a settler tracked Caesar to his camp and demanded his surrender. Caesar raised his gun but the settler was quicker. Caesar was fatally wounded and soon died. Unlike later bushrangers, Caesar was never reported to have killed anyone.

ASSIGNMENT OR GOVERNMENT WORK

When Phillip was Governor, convicts worked on government farms, made bricks, and erected public buildings; and partly looked after themselves. He had suggested to the British Government that officers might be encouraged to start farms if they were given grants of land and assigned one or two convicts to work as farm labourers. When permission for this was granted, Grose not only gave 40 hectares of land to every officer who asked for it, but he also provided each with ten convicts as labourers and another three as servants. While Grose was in charge, the cost of clothing and feeding these convicts was also paid by the colony.

With different governors, and with changes in the British Government, many alterations were made to the assignment system. But the principle remained the same. Whenever convicts arrived in the colony, except for tradesmen (also called mechanics or artificers) who were used by the authorities, the first selection was made by the settlers needing labour.

Later settlers were supposed to pay the colony for the services of such men, or they had to provide them with food and clothing. Whatever happened, the British Government was always determined that the colony and its convicts should not cost a penny more than was necessary.

A convict's future life depended largely on his master. The lucky ones could become contented farm workers. They wore the clothes of an ordinary labourer and were well fed and housed; they were also allowed luxuries such as sugar and tobacco.

One man wrote home: "All a man has got to mind is to keep a still tongue in his head and do his master's duty; but if he don't, he may as well be hung at once, for they would send you to the magistrates and get 100 lashes, and then get sent to a place called Port Arthur to work in irons for two or three years."

But on the farms of poor settlers, or greedy ones, food was strictly rationed, the assigned convict might have to sleep in a leaking hut and was lucky to be given any bedding.

Convicts on government work in the early days were given a task for a day. When this was completed they could earn money. Until 1819, when Macquarie built four convict barracks, they had to find their own place to sleep. Some paid rent for a space in a slab hut with other convicts; others lived in outhouses owned by emancipists (convicts who had been pardoned or served their term) or free settlers.

The only shelter provided by the government in the early days was for hardened criminals who worked in the chain gangs.

TAMING THE UNREPENTANT

Throughout the period of transportation, there were always men who refused to obey the rules and could not be "tamed". To cope with them, several "secondary punishment" settlements were established. At these, treatment was the most severe that could be imagined and the authorities' aim was to make death preferable to being sent to such a place.

Those in Tasmania included Macquarie Harbour (1821-22), Maria Island (1825-32 and 1842-50), and Port Arthur (1830-77). In New South Wales there were Norfolk Island (particularly from 1826-56) and Port Macquarie (1821-47).

The first of these "hells on earth" was at Newcastle in New South Wales. Coal was discovered near Newcastle NSW in 1791 and Australia's first export of coal was shipped to the Cape of Good Hope in 1801. The penal settlement was formed in June 1801. The convicts, in irons, worked naked in mine shafts often no more than a metre high. They were flogged on the least pretext.

A still worse task was lime-burning. To make mortar, teams of convicts often in double irons and with their backs raw from the "cat", had to crush and burn oyster shells so that there would always be "1200 bushels" of lime ready for shipment to Sydney. When the boats

arrived, baskets of unslaked lime were carried out on the prisoners' backs. They were naked save for the smallest apron and any spilled lime badly seared their partly healed lash wounds.

When it was decided that Newcastle was too close to Sydney and there were too many escapes from Port Macquarie, farther north in NSW, another penal settlement was formed at Moreton Bay in 1824. During the 20 years of its existence, 2259 men and 144 women convicts were sent to this sub-tropical hell. At Moreton Bay, the overseers were really brutal as was the most notorious commandant,

Captain Patrick Logan, who was later killed by the Aborigines.

The treadmill was the particular instrument of torture there. Up to 25 prisoners could work it to grind maize, but for punishment only 16, each wearing heavy shackles, had to work on it for 14 hours. Four men at a time could take a break, but the other 12 had to keep the wheel turning. Any man who could not keep pace had his shins sharply hit by the next tread. Any attempt to slow the pace was stopped by the overseer's "cat". In the high temperatures, men often fainted and fell off.

TWO GOVERNORS

Arthur

In Australian slang, Lieutenant-Governor George Arthur, who ruled Van Diemen's Land (Tasmania) from 1824 to 1836, was a "wowser". He believed that any type of amusement was the work of the devil.

Although the men in his prisons were given adequate food and clothes, he rewarded only those who showed improvement.

At Port Arthur, his escape-proof prison near Hobart, convicts were kept working from dawn to dusk. Rules were read to them once a week and even failure to salute an officer could be punished with a flogging. Other offences were punished by making them wear heavy chains while cutting and carting timber or mining coal. No convict was allowed any private possessions and most were forbidden tobacco and all articles of luxury.

On Sundays, convicts attended two church services; after work they had to attend evening classes.

When asked what he thought of convicts and emancipists being allowed to mix with free settlers, Arthur said, "I think it is impossible that such a class of persons can be residents in any country without the most polluting consequences".

George Arthur

Maconochie

When Captain Alexander Maconochie, a former naval officer, arrived at Norfolk Island in 1840, he found "a turbulent, brutal hell". Instead of forcing convicts to endure punishment for the least mistake, he introduced a system of marks for good behaviour. He believed that discipline should be relaxed gradually so that prisoners might learn to resist temptation.

Instead of forcing them to eat, several at a time with their bare hands from buckets beside the toilets, he gave prisoners cutlery and allowed them to eat off plates.

On the Queen's Birthday in 1840, all 1800 prisoners were "free" for the day. After dinner, they were given a tot of rum to toast the Queen. Then they had an afternoon of sports. This was followed by a play which was accompanied by music and songs that "contributed to the hilarity".

Some convicts misused Maconochie's privileges, and his scheme was too expensive for the government. However, he showed that some of the most hardened criminals could respond favourably when treated like human beings.

Prisoners having a rest

19

THE LOOK OF A CONVICT

Most drawings and sketches of convicts show faces which look like the grotesque people in the paintings of Breughel and the cartoons of Hogarth.

Did the effects of the penal system cause these men to look different? Some people certainly thought that they did.

In 1842, when David Burn visited Port Arthur, he wrote: "It was hideous to remark on the countenances of the men, to which their yellow raiment (or half black, half yellow), with P.A. (Port

Arthur), and their respective numbers stamped on various parts, imparted a sinister and most revolting expression. Scarcely one set of open features were to be found. Crime and its consequences were fearfully depicted in their visages and we turned from the disagreeable caricature of humanity with as much disgust as pity and regret." And yet Burn felt that he had to add, "However disagreeable to its constrained visitors, we found Port Arthur a place of beauty, kindness, courtesy and goodwill".

Sir Roger Therry, a judge, wrote of some men who had returned from two or three years on Norfolk Island, "Their sunken glazed eyes, deathly pale faces, hollow fleshless cheeks, and once manly limbs, shrivelled and withered up as if by premature old age, created a thrill of horror amongst the bystanders. They were all under 35 years of age. There was not one who had not, from time to time, undergone a punishment of 1000 lashes each and upwards."

One convict artist confirmed that convicts were thought to be different. Thomas Griffiths Wainewright (1794-1847) was transported to Tasmania in 1827. After serving in the chain gang and as a hospital warder he was given ticket-of-leave. Although made to sleep in the convict barracks, he was allowed to move about Hobart so that he could paint flattering portraits of the wealthy citizens and officials.

Among his sketches is a self-portrait. Below the drawing of a face which seems quite normal, he wrote "Head of a *Convict,* very characteristic of *low cunning and revenge*"!

Head of a Convict, very characteristic of low cunning & revenge!

FINAL DAYS OF AN OCEAN HELL

After Maconochie left Norfolk Island in 1844, conditions returned to those of an "ocean hell". Prisoners brought there from Sydney had to swim ashore if it was too rough to launch a boat, and often several drowned.

Each man was issued with a "frock" of cotton duck, trousers, a coarse shirt and a straw hat. He was given a coarse woollen jacket for the cooler months, but no shoes were provided.

In 1845, convicts were still kept short of food. Hominy ("maize meal and water boiled to the consistency of baked rice pudding, which it resembled only in appearance" and sweetened with half an ounce of sugar a day) was all they got for breakfast and supper. Dinner was little better: "A morsel of salt junk (meat) very like old saddle" and "nauseous, coarse, maize bread tasting as if it were composed of sawdust".

While the military officers amused themselves with "picnics, shooting, boating and flirting", the convicts were kept hard at work hoeing the paddocks. Strict convict overseers watched them by day and night and complained to the superintendent if any rule was broken.

Punishment was mostly flogging (from 50-300 lashes), but what all prisoners dreaded was solitary confinement in the "black hole". This was an underground cell, entered by an overhead trapdoor

which was then covered to keep out the light. Men left there alone for 30, 60 or 90 days were driven mad by the silence and darkness.

Others who committed further crimes (or annoyed the overseers) could be sentenced to wearing double irons while working in the stone quarry under a blazing sun.

What must have been the ultimate torture was that as these half-starved prisoners went to their places of work, they passed all sorts of fruit — pineapples, guavas, bananas flanked by hedges of sugar cane — in the officers' gardens. The paddocks were filled with sweet potatoes and their gaolers and their families ate fresh meat.

Only prisoners given special privileges, such as teaching an officer's children, might be allowed to walk about the island. Occasionally one might find some wild fruit. While an officer could brew coffee from beans grown in his own garden, a "trusty" could make a substitute by burning maize meal on a shovel. Such men also baked an improved bread by mixing sweet potato with the maize meal. The officers, of course, had bread made from wheat flour.

HULKS IN VICTORIA

Although an attempt was made in 1803 to establish a colony in what is now known as Victoria, there was no real settlement for another 30 years. In 1834-35, the Henty family moved from Tasmania to settle at Portland Bay, and John Batman and John Pascoe Fawkner settled in the Port Phillip Bay area.

In the 1840s, the British Government devised a new form of transportation.

Anyone sentenced to be transported first served some time in a British gaol. Then they would be sent to Australia where they could live and work as free men and women; but convicts could not return home until they had fully served their sentence. Such exiles saved the British and colonial governments part of the cost of their upkeep. They were named "Pentonvillains" after the new Pentonville prison in London. The first arrived at Port Phillip in 1844. Similar men

on conditional pardons (and some escapees) came from Tasmania. But by August 1849, there was so much opposition to transportation that when the convict transport ship *Randolph* arrived in Port Phillip Bay, the Governor, Charles Joseph La Trobe refused to allow any of the convicts to land.

However, Victoria was not free from crime. During the early 1850s thousands of migrants had gone to the newly discovered goldfields and some form of prison had to be established for those who broke the law.

Again the solution was the "hulks". In 1852, five ships deserted by crews who had gone to seek gold were taken over by the government and rebuilt to house criminals. Prisoners sentenced to live on these vessels, which lay moored in Hobson's Bay, included most of the worst offenders. One of the most infamous was the bushranger "Mad" Dan Morgan.

Conditions aboard the hulks varied. The most desperate prisoners were confined in airless cells below water level except for an hour a day when they were marched up and down the deck. All convicts serving a sentence of two years or more were put in irons which weighed from 7 to 20kg. Those taken ashore to work on road gangs or in quarries still had to wear these irons.

The hulks were guarded continually by armed sentries. Yet some men weighted with leg irons jumped overboard seeking death. Any man who survived received an additional punishment — a heavy ball of iron weighing 35kg attached by a chain to his belt.

Altogether, 5128 prisoners spent periods aboard the hulks. In 1857, when 80 prisoners working ashore murdered the Inspector of Penal Settlements, there were public protests and conditions aboard the hulks were revealed. They were removed in 1858.

THE TARDY WEST

A few convicts were sent with the troops who established the first Western Australian outpost at Albany in the late 1820s. But when the colony was proclaimed in 1829, Captain James Stirling announced that this would be the first colony of free men in Australia.

During the next 20 years, 4500 new settlers migrated to the west. Many, however, found the promises made in Britain about the new colony to be inaccurate. By 1849, only 2000 hectares of land were being cultivated and there were not enough labourers to build the essential public buildings in Perth, the capital.

In 1849, when colonists in eastern Australia were clamouring for an end to transportation, the people of Perth demanded that the British Government allow them to establish a large-scale penal settlement to provide low-cost labour.

The British, again suffering from over-populated prisons, were happy to oblige. In 1850 the first shipment of 75 convicts arrived to find that there was not even accommodation for them. They were the forerunners of 9700 men (no women

Left: Fremantle Gaol
Below: The Settlement at King
George Sound, 1827

prisoners were sent to Western Australia) who arrived during the next 28 years. Unlike those in eastern Australia, the convicts who were sent to the west received much better treatment. Most were less than 45 years old and many arrived to be granted an immediate ticket-of-leave. People holding a ticket-of-leave were forbidden to enter South Australia and Victoria. Many could live only by going to a government depot, where they could get work as labourers. One man who gained such freedom to earn his own living, applied for a hawker's licence only to find it refused because such occupations had been banned. But the only requirements on his release were that he had to be home by 10p.m. and report twice a year to the police.

Convicts sent to work in country centres had a relatively easy time, even when working with road gangs. The food was good, the men were allowed to keep pets, and had books to read from the prison library.

No convict in Western Australia was assigned to any private settler, so none could be at the mercy of their masters. The punishment was never cruel, vindictive or harsh as it was at Port Arthur, Norfolk Island and similar penal settlements.

ONE CONVICT'S LIFE

Few of the convicts transported to Australia could read and write, but one who did record his experiences was a gentleman, J.F. Mortlock, who wrote *Experiences of a Convict*.

Mortlock believed that his family had been cheated of a legacy and he made various attempts to expose the wickedness of his uncles. Finally, in 1842, he tried to frighten one uncle by shooting a blank cartridge at him in his room at Christ's College, Cambridge.

Mortlock, who was then 32 years old was tried for attempted murder and sentenced to twenty-one years' transportation.

He was first taken to the hulks at Portsmouth, where he spent eighteen weeks in irons. In December 1843, he was transported to Norfolk Island just when the successor to Governor Maconochie was re-imposing severe conditions.

Later Mortlock was sent to Tasmania where he had to cut timber and clear land on the Tasman Peninsula. Because he was

well behaved, he was allowed to work as a constable, a school teacher and as clerk of a road gang. Mortlock was granted a ticket-of-leave in 1852 and recommended for a conditional pardon two years later. He travelled throughout Tasmania as a pedlar or hawker for several years.

Although free within Australia, Mortlock was not allowed to return to England. Despite this he went back in 1857 and after his arrival he was arrested again. He was imprisoned in England for a year and then returned to Australia to complete his twenty-one years' sentence.

In 1859 he arrived in Western Australia where treatment of the convicts was much more lenient than he had previously experienced. After working on a road gang and finally receiving his pardon, Mortlock again became a hawker in Tasmania. Later he visited the Victorian goldfields. He legally returned to England in 1864.

Despite his efforts, he never received the legacy he claimed was his. He died in England in 1882, as poor as he had been in life, leaving property worth £154-18-1.

THE AFTER EFFECTS

How successful was the transportation system for the people who were sent to Australia?

In many ways it was a gamble. Men assigned to cruel masters, or who annoyed a particular overseer, might just as well have been dead.

If they were sent to the most dreaded penal settlements at Newcastle, Moreton Bay, Macquarie Harbour, Port Arthur or Norfolk Island, they could have been driven mad. If not, many deliberately did something which they knew would result in death — either by hanging or suicide.

Most of the men who escaped and became bushrangers had a very short period of freedom before they were shot while being hunted, or hanged after a trial.

And yet, even Governor Arthur claimed that of the 17 000 convicts transported to Van Diemen's Land from 1804 to 1836, 5000 never had another complaint made against them.

George St, Sydney 1829

Governor Hunter said that after he returned to England, emancipists who had gone "home" often approached him saying that they could make a better life in Australia.

Except for a few well-known individuals who completed their sentences or were pardoned, and then achieved wealth and fame, the others avoided the public gaze. They did not want any more trouble and no one knows how many chose to remain in Australia and live quiet family lives.

Others who were released, reverted to the life that they had known in the slums of England. In the *Australian* newspaper of 1829, there were descriptions of Sydney streets being so filled with drunken brawling prostitutes that "a decent woman could not venture through the streets without having her modesty shocked by the victims of colonial depravity".

But the native-born "currency lads", the children of convicts, were said to be sober and honest. It was they who made a real contribution to Australia, and their attitudes which have had a great influence in forming the personality of today's Australians.

GLOSSARY

assignment: a method of providing convicts to work as labourers for military and early settlers in Australia

"cat" (or cat-o'-nine-tails): a whip with nine "tails" or lashes, each knotted at the end, sometimes with a piece of metal in each knot

chain gang: a gang or group of convicts, each chained to the next man, or each wearing heavy chains and shackles which stopped all but the least movement

"currency lads" (and lasses): free-born children of convicts, born and reared in Australia

emancipist: a convict who had served his or her sentence, or had been pardoned

hulks: ships, no longer fit to be used at sea, which were refitted as floating prisons for convicts, both in England and Australia

irons (and double-irons): heavy bands of metal fitted around the ankles and other parts of the body. Originally designed to prevent escape, a man could be "loaded" with irons as an extra punishment. The bands were usually joined by chains between ankles, waist and wrists

lash: another name for the "cat-o'-nine tails"

to pick oakum: to untwist and sort tarred rope ends which were then used to prevent leaks between planks on ships. Usually done as punishment by women convicts

shackles: rings around the wrists and/or ankles, often joined together with a chain. *(See also* irons)

slab hut: crude type of building made by early settlers using thick planks of roughly cut timber as walls. They were buried into the earth and attached to beams

slops: name for loose clothing issued to convicts by government, usually of distinctive colour or with numbers and/or arrows

ticket-of-leave: freedom given to a convict to live and work in a certain area provided he/she reported regularly to the authorities

transportation: a form of punishment, given instead of a death sentence, whereby a convict was sent by ship (transported) to a penal colony outside the country where he/she committed the offence. All early convicts sent from England to Australia were "transported"

treadmill: a form of punishment which forced prisoners to walk non-stop for many hours

THE OFFICIAL
WEST HAM UNITED
ANNUAL 2006

WEST HAM UNITED

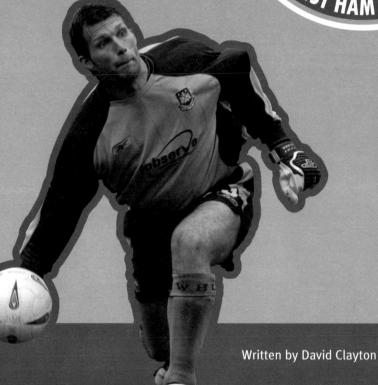

Written by David Clayton

A Grange Publication
© 2005. Published by Grange Communications Ltd.,
Edinburgh, under licence from West Ham United
Football Club. Printed in the EU.

Photographs © Action Images

ISBN 1-905426-05-4

£6.99

CONTENTS

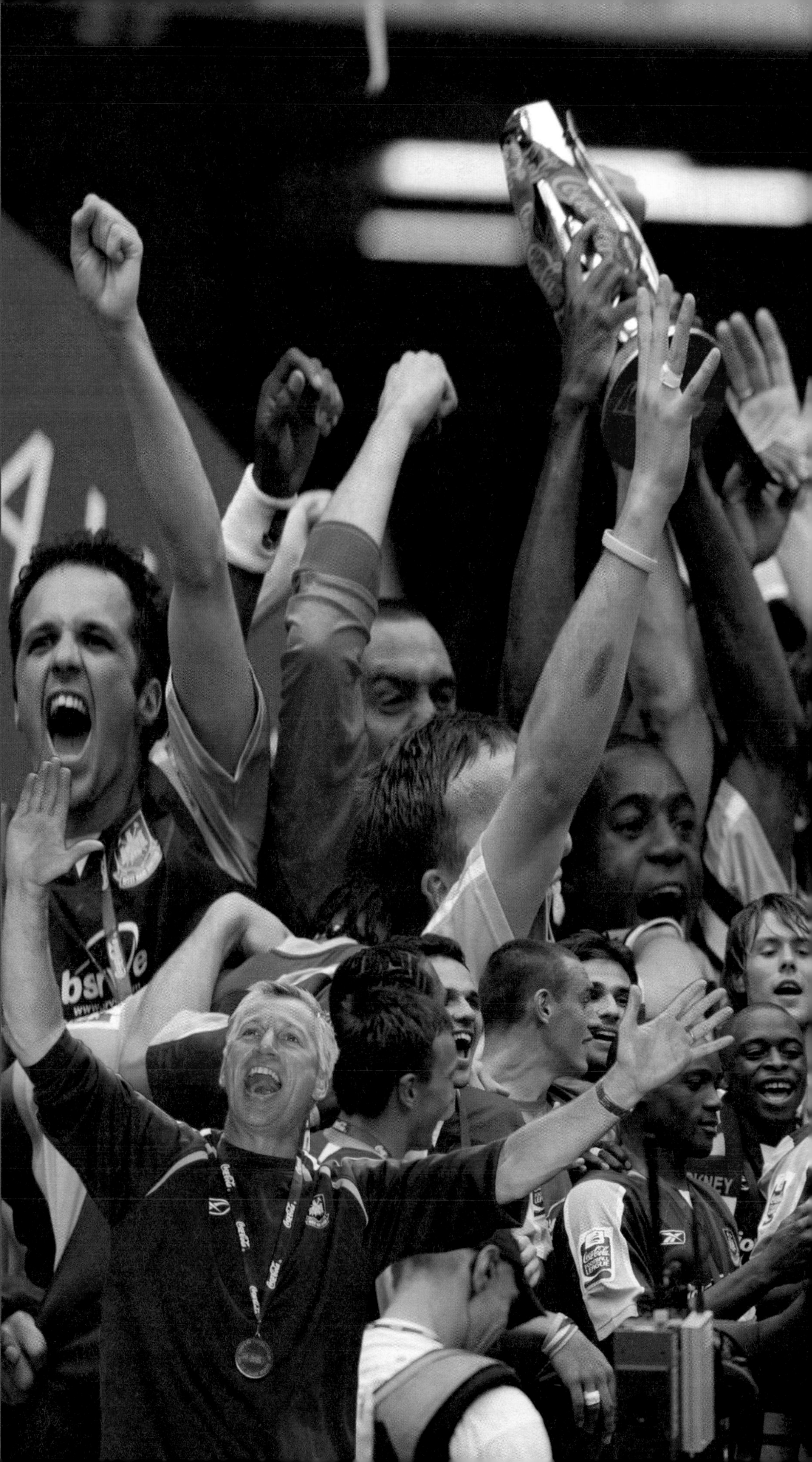

WELCOME!

Welcome to the West Ham Annual 2006! We hope you enjoy looking back over last season and ahead to what looks like an exciting campaign for 2005/6 with the Hammers back where they belong in the Premiership. There is an exciting season ahead and it will be fantastic to see some of Europe's biggest stars visit Upton Park again.

Alan Pardew has added to the squad that won promotion and will have his team pumped up and ready for 38 cup finals in the coming months. With our fantastic support, there's no reason it shouldn't be a thoroughly enjoyable campaign.

In the following pages we look back at the epic 2004/05 season, culminating with a special feature on the play-off final with Preston.

We also focus on the manager, Teddy Sheringham, Mark Noble, Matthew Etherington, Nigel Reo-Coker and Roy Carroll, as well as profile every member of the first team squad.

There are lots of quizzes, puzzles plus a crossword and wordsearch to keep you busy plus facts about the club's history. So get your thinking caps on and remember – no cheating by looking at the answers page at the back! Enjoy the Annual and keep cheering the Hammers on – **the best team in the land!**

MANAGER
ALAN PARDEW

Good Enough!

It has not been an easy road for Alan Pardew since he became West Ham manager. In fact, it's been quite a turbulent couple of years for the former Crystal Palace hero with the Hammers fans' expections high and the desire to return to the Premiership growing stronger each extra minute West Ham were out of it.

There were periods when results weren't going right and the team couldn't buy a home win – but Pardew stuck by his beliefs and remained strong throughout and ultimately, who could have blamed the Hammers' young boss if he'd looked like the cat that had got the cream last May in Cardiff?

Of course, he didn't look like that and his reaction was dignified and calm. He'd done what he'd set out to achieve and now he will lead the club and continue his good work in the Premiership.

Escaping The Championship was never going to be easy, especially when there were perhaps a dozen teams all as good as each other and battling for the three available promotion slots. In fact, from the top of the division to the bottom, all sides seemed capable of beating each other and the race to stay in the hunt was all about consistency.

Pardew never doubted his team's ability and despite constant media speculation, he rose above the snipers to show what a promising manager he is. He moved into the coaching side of the game at Barnet and then moved to Reading to take charge of the reserve team in 1997, a position he held until the end of the 1998/99 season. The reserve team at Reading

THE BOSS

was then disbanded but within a couple of months, Pardew was invited back to the Royals, who were all set to move into the swanky new Madjeski Stadium – but this time as manager of the first team.

He steered them back to the First Division in 2002 and they made it to the play-off semi finals 12 months later. At the start of 2003/04 Reading were again among the leaders but West Ham's interest proved too great a distraction for Pardew who resigned from his post at the Madjeski in September. He was forced to wait another month before he officially started as the Hammers' boss, taking over on October 18, 2003 from caretaker boss Trevor Brooking.

He almost took his new side to the Premiership at the first attempt, only to lose 1-0 to Crystal Palace in the play-off final. His second season – his first full campaign as boss – was full of ups, downs and injuries, but the Hammers stayed in sixth position longer than any other club over the course of the season and so deservedly took their place in the play-offs in May. Now Pardew will begin with a clean slate and aim to show the football world that West Ham's rightful place is among the Premiership elite, playing football the way it's meant to be played.

WELL DONE PARDS!

HAMMER OF THE YEAR 2004/2005

SWEET SHERI!

Few footballers can maintain the high standards they set at the peak of their careers, especially as they enter the veteran stage of their careers. But intelligence, technique and vision rarely leave gifted players, whatever age they are, even though advancing years can obviously affect fitness and stamina.

There are a few exceptions to this rule, apart from goalkeepers who have different demands on their bodies. Billy Bonds springs to mind, as does Stuart Pearce – two seasoned campaigners that outlasted many of their age groups – and now add Teddy Sheringham to that list.

Teddy will celebrate his 40th birthday during the latter half of the 2005/06 campaign and will likely be the oldest player in the Premiership this season. But as he proved last year, with 21 goals from 28 starts, some players are like vintage wine – they just seem to get better with age!

A boyhood Hammers fan, Teddy's career began many years ago, not too far down the road at Millwall, where he would become a huge crowd favourite during his six years in the first team. He was then transferred to Nottingham Forest for £2million but failed to settle in the East Midlands and was soon off to Spurs for £3.5million, winning the Golden Boot in 1993 for his 29 league goals.

He also formed an excellent partnership with Alan Shearer for England and Teddy's two goals in the 4-1 win over Holland during Euro 96 will be fondly remembered by many for years to come.

A couple of years later he was signed by Manchester United to fill the boots of the departed Eric Cantona – though this was an unenviable task, he eventually found his form for United and was an integral part of their 1999 treble which included the Champions League, Premiership and FA Cup – ironically, his first silverware all arrived within the space of a month!

In 2001 he returned to Spurs for another successful couple of years before being allowed to join former Hammers boss Harry Redknapp at Portsmouth. Teddy duly banged four goals in for Pompey on his debut! When it was clear he would be available in the summer of 2004, Alan Pardew moved quickly to bring him to Upton Park to help steer his young side in the right direction.

Teddy was an inspiration during his first season in Claret and Blue and was voted Hammer of the Year for 2005. Injury cost him his place on the promotion run-in but as soon as the season was over, Pardew offered Teddy a new one-year deal, which, thankfully, he signed.

This could be his last year as a player but you can bet he will be giving it his all to make sure it's a happy end to a magnificent career – but you never know – if he plays this season like he did during 2004/05, maybe he could be persuaded....

11

BACK
WHERE WE BELONG!

SEASON 2004/05 REVIEW

After just missing out in the 2003/04 play-off final, Alan Pardew's side had to do it all again in a bid for Premiership football...

It was difficult for players and fans alike to contemplate another 10-month slog in the newly-christened Coca-Cola Championship after the heartbreak of losing to Crystal Palace at the Millennium Stadium, but that's exactly what they had to do.

Sitting back and feeling sorry for ourselves was not about to solve a thing and only hard work, belief and a sprinkling of luck would enable the Hammers to seriously challenge for promotion again. The first few games of the 2004/05 campaign were crucial and would shape the coming months.

There were a few squad changes too, with experienced Rob Lee, Kevin Horlock, Brian Deane and David Connolly all leaving Upton Park while Luke Chadwick, Jimmy Walker, Sergei Rebrov and the evergreen Teddy Sheringham were drafted in.

The season began with a tough trip to relegated Leicester City but both sides cancelled each other – and ended with 10 men after Rufus Brevett and Dion Dublin were sent off – in an acceptable 0-0 draw. Sheringham opened his account in the first home match against Reading three days later, scoring the only goal in a 1-0 win.

Wigan Athletic then travelled to the Boleyn Ground and the home defence was led a merry dance by Jason Roberts and Nathan Ellington as the visitors left with a 3-1 win – Bobby Zamora scoring a consolation goal. Four points from nine was not the start everyone had hoped for and the loss of Christian Dailly through injury and then Michael Carrick to Spurs were bitter pills to swallow for the supporters but life had to go on.

A first away league win of the season was needed to lift everybody and a trip to Crewe offered that chance. Thankfully a scintillating first half display that saw two goals from Sheringham and another from Brevett virtually killed the game before the break. Crewe pulled a couple back but the game ended 3-2. A 2-0 Carling Cup win over Southend followed by a 1-0 over Burnley and the campaign suddenly had a very different look about it with just one defeat in six plus four clean sheets in the bank, plus a place in the top six.

SEASON 2004/05 REVIEW

'05

A feature of the Hammers' season, however, would be inconsistency and they suffered a 2-1 loss at Coventry, despite being ahead. Carl Fletcher was signed for £250,000 from Bournemouth to bolster the squad and an impressive 2-1 win at Sheffield United, thanks to a cracking goal from Marlon Harewood and a deflected Sheringham free kick was a huge boost. Then followed a hard-fought 1-0 win over Rotherham, which put Pardew's side up to fourth in the table. A 1-1 draw at home to leaders Ipswich Town included a Sheringham penalty miss at 1-0 and a stunning miss by Harewood was not a disaster. Further progress in the Carling Cup followed with a 3-2 win over Notts County (which included another penalty miss – this time by Zamora). Things were going steadily if not spectacularly at Upton Park.

But just one point from six was taken from visits to Nottingham Forest (1-2) and Derby (1-1) and the up and down results continued with a 1-0 win over Wolves, a 1-0 loss to QPR and successive wins over Stoke (2-0) and Gillingham (3-1). The Hammers were back up to fourth and right back in the thick of the action again – if the frustrating dropped points against seemingly lesser sides could be eradicated, a top two finish was surely possible.

One of the highlights of the season so far was a trip to Stamford Bridge to take on Chelsea in the Carling Cup. With 6,000 travelling fans giving the Hammers fantastic support, Chelsea were somewhat fortunate to edge the game 1-0 through Kezman.

1 Who scored the first goal of the 2004/05 campaign and who supplied the cross?

2 Who was sent off against Burnley at Upton Park and what was the final score?

3 Which three players signed prior to the 2-1 win at Sheffield United last season and which of the trio didn't make their debut?

4 Who said this: *"It's tough because I find this year whenever I am getting the ball I have two players on me – so it's harder to get into the game. It's something I have to deal with and I just have to get on with it."*

5 Who scored the first and last goals of West Ham's 2004/05 season?

6 Who was Alan Pardew talking about and why when he said: "This is one of the most honest acts from a player I have experienced in all my years in the game."

7 Who did the Hammers beat on New Year's Day 2005 and by what score? What was notable about the goals scored?

8 Who joined Nottingham Forest on loan in February 2005?

9 Who was named Most Improved Young Player for season 2004/05?

10 Who said this after the play-off final win over Preston: *"It's a dream come true. I'm a local lad and there were loads of my friends and family at the Millennium and just to win and be part of the team that got the Club back to the Premier League – it's just unbelieveable."*

SEASON 2004/05 REVIEW

Back in the league, long trips to Plymouth and Cardiff yielded just one point and a thrashing in Wales where Cardiff triumphed 4-1. More mixed fortunes in successive games at Upton Park with two Harewood efforts securing a 2-1 win over QPR but lowly Brighton left with a shock 1-0 win – a result repeated in the next game, a single goal loss to Millwall.

Defeat at home to Watford was unthinkable but after 20 minutes the Hammers trailed 2-0! But the game was far from over and a thrilling fight back ended with Rebrov scoring the fifth and final goal of the game and completing a 3-2 win for the hosts. A terrific 2-0 win at Sunderland with goals from leading scorers Harewood and Sheringham kept West Ham in fifth but frustratingly, just one win in the next four games a 3-2 Boxing Day win over Nottingham Forest – saw us slip out of the play-off places for the first time since August.

The points dropped at Preston (1-2) and draws against Leeds and Rotherham, two games that should have been won, put extra pressure on the manager and players to get something out of the visit to leaders Ipswich on New Year's Day. Fortunately, we got it, with a fine 2-0 win – Ipswich's first home defeat of the season.

But a 2-0 home loss to Sheffield United cancelled out the optimism. The Hammers just couldn't string a winning run together and the nerve endings were already jangling. The FA Cup victory over Norwich was a welcome break from the pressures of league action with Harewood's strike seeing off the Premiership strugglers but successive league defeats to Wolves and Derby saw the Irons drop to ninth.

Yet just when it seemed things were going wrong, positive results turned things back around – a narrow last-minute 1-0 win over Cardiff was followed by an emphatic 5-0 over Plymouth. For the first time in the season, the winning streak became three in a row with a 1-0 win at Gillingham putting us back in fifth towards the end of February.

Nobody was too worried with the FA Cup fourth round exit to Sheffield United (after a replay) but just when things seemed to be going well in the league, a terribly timed run of poor form struck. Defeats at Leeds and at home to Preston were followed by a crushing 3-1 loss at Reading yet the Hammers were still within sight of a play-off spot. Shaun Newton arrived on loan from Wolves, initially to replace the suspended Tomas Repka but he would later sign a permanent deal.

It looked like a morale-boosting win over Crewe was on the cards until the visitors stole a last-gasp equaliser. A 2-2 draw with Leicester hardly improved matters but at least the odd point was still being added to the total. With difficult games at Wigan and Burnley next up, the Hammers needed maximum points to stay in with a play-off chance – and they got them! Wigan were dispatched 2-1 and Burnley 1-0, followed by a 3-0 win over Coventry City. Those nine points could not have come at a better time – but there were still plenty of nervy matches to come!

Draws against Millwall and Brighton were sandwiched by a 1-0 win at Stoke and it was the Hammers' form on the road that was keeping us in the hunt at the top. With two games left it was touch and go whether West Ham would feature in the play-off semis and if results went against them elsewhere, it would be impossible.

One home game was left – against champions Sunderland – plus a visit to Watford. Sunderland proved too good on the day and won 2-1, despite being 1-0 down to a Harewood strike, meaning anything but a win at Vicarage Road and the Hammers would spend their third successive season outside the Premiership. With Teddy Sheringham ruled out through injury, many wondered whether the Hammers' chance had gone.

Watford had nothing to play for but pride and Anton Ferdinand's volley sent almost 5,000 travelling fans wild. Harewood's penalty secured victory despite a late flourish from the home side and a 2-1 win meant the Hammers had finished sixth and faced Ipswich Town for a place in the play-off final.

Having taken four points off Ipswich already, confidence was high and Pardew's side raced into a 2-0 lead in the first half of the first leg but Ipswich were far from finished and came back to claim a 2-2 draw. It established them as favourites to progress to the final – but Bobby Zamora had other ideas.

GOOD GAME!

**MAY 30, 2005, MILLENNIUM STADIUM
COCA-COLA CHAMPIONSHIP PLAY-OFF FINAL
WEST HAM 1, PRESTON 0**

Nobody underestimated Preston North End following two 2-1-league defeats to the north-west outfit. Preston had secured a play-off place two months before the Hammers did but on paper, it was West Ham who had the greater experience of big occasions such as this, though Teddy Sheringham's fitness meant he was left on the bench.

Jimmy Walker was preferred to Stephen Bywater in goal while Bobby Zamora and Marlon Harewood led the attack. More than 70,000 fans were in attendance as the game kicked off with the prize of a place in the Premiership at stake.

The Hammers began brightly with Shaun Newton putting Tomas Repka in with a chance early on but the Czech star, who had never scored in 165 previous appearances for the Irons, saw his shot smack the post. Then Matty Etherington forced Carlo Nash into a great save – that was the last real chance before half-time and the teams went in 0-0 at the break.

Then Nigel Reo-Coker put Harewood clear only for Nash to save well and Zamora then saw his follow-up shot cleared off the line and Harewood's second attempt was again saved by the keeper. But the pressure finally paid off when Etherington's cross found Zamora who volleyed home to send the Hammers fans wild.

But there was still drama to come!

A long cross towards the West Ham box saw Jimmy Walker misjudge his positioning and try to re-adjust in mid-air as he caught the ball outside the box. The result was an horrific knee injury that left the former Walsall man in agony on the ground.

Stephen Bywater came on as a substitute and his first job was to keep out a Preston free-kick. Moments later the referee blew for time and the celebrations really began. It was the culmination of a rollercoaster season and just reward for manager Alan Pardew and his team, who had been the subject of criticism at various points of the campaign.

For the fans, it was a dream come true. The Hammers – back in the big time – back in the Premiership, where, of course, we belong!

TOP 10 GOALS

The best strikes of the season – as voted for by Hammers fans – but before Bobby Zamora's wonderful volley at Ipswich, which may well have won it – better luck next year Bobby!

1 MARLON HAREWOOD V SHEFFIELD UNITED 11/9/04

Picking the ball up 40 yards out, Harewood controlled the ball and then sent an unstoppable shot past the Sheffield keeper for a spectacular goal.

2 TEDDY SHERINGHAM V CREWE 15/3/05

A free-kick was awarded 25 yards from goal. Sheringham judged the wall and the position of the Crewe keeper before stepping up to delightfully curl the ball into the top right-hand corner.

3 MARLON HAREWOOD V GILLINGHAM 23/10/04

Etherington played the ball to the edge of the Gillingham box to Zamora who spotted Harewood's dash into the six-yard box and the former Forest striker finished powerfully as he slid in.

4 GAVIN WILLIAMS V LEEDS UNITED 26/2/05

A pass into Sheringham was chested down by the former England striker into the path of Gavin Williams who controlled it on his thigh and volleyed it with style into the roof of the net from 18 yards.

5 MARLON HAREWOOD V MILLWALL 16/4/05

A great move began with Chris Powell finding Etherington who cut inside and played a one-two with Sheringham and then crossed the ball to Harewood who finished neatly from near the penalty spot.

6 TEDDY SHERINGHAM V WOLVES 2/10/04

The move began with Sheringham laying the ball off to Harewood who attempted to play Etherington through. The pass was cut out but Sheringham picked up the loose ball, skipping one challenge before tucking the ball past the Wolves keeper from 20 yards out.

7 MATTHEW ETHERINGTON V ROTHERHAM 14/9/04

The Hammers were awarded a free-kick on the edge of the Rotherham box with the scores locked at 0-0. Etherington stepped up to curl a low curling drive into the net from 20 yards for the winning goal.

8 SERGEI REBROV V WATFORD 27/11/04

With the scores at 2-2, the ball was crossed into the Watford box by Matty Etherington and sliding in at the far post was Sergei Rebrov to finish with a low drive and seal three points.

9 ADAM NOWLAND V BURNLEY 28/8/04

Hayden Mullins sent in a deep cross into the Burnley box and the ball was cleared to the edge of the box where the on-rushing Adam Nowland connected with a powerful shot into the ground which gave the keeper no chance.

10 BOBBY ZAMORA V PRESTON 5/3/05

Marlon Harewood ran down the left, checked inside and then picked out Bobby Zamora at the far post. The former Brighton man volleyed home with style for a terrific goal.

WORDSEARCH

Figure out what words the clues represent. Then find the words in the grid.
Words can go horizontally, vertically and diagonally in all eight directions.

```
K J T H W P L P R W X B G D
R E J P R E S T O N T T N B
T C K L T L M L T N W U K X
B R K B H E V Z P T O F H N
C A K M L E R R Q R Z T X H
Y E N B S A L A G K G L K V
B P R K P D C N L N H L B D
S T M Y J H Y K I C R L U T
N R G C R E C K B M L R B J
O A N K L J O L T U K T B X
R U Y O N O D L X R R M L T
I T B T R V M X Z R L N E N
X S L B W K W T H H Q R S X
D O O W E R A H N O L R A M
```

CLUES

1. Former West Ham favourite now manager at Manchester City (6,6) ✓

2. Name of Hammers, ground (6,6)   *Boleyn ground* ✓

3. North End, team beaten in the play-off 2005 final (7) ✓

4. Opening opponents of 2005/06 (9)

5. They are pretty and float in the sky (7) ✓   *bubbles* ✓

6. Hungry like the _____ - Shaun Newton's former club (6)

7. He found his way out of the Forest (6,8)

8. Our home colours - _____ and blue (6)   *claret* ✓

9. One of our two nicknames (5)   *irons* ✓

10. Legendary former player Trevor, now working for the FA (8)   *Brooking*

NAME GAME

Work out the Hammers star by solving these anagrams...

1 BROKEN LAM

2 **STAMP ARE OK**

3 **MADE SHY NUN ILL**

4 WHALED KICK U C

5 **DONNER NAAN RIFT**

6 IS HANG DRY THEMED

7 **ROCK LINE GEORGE**

8 LO CAR LORRY

Bobby Zamora

9 **BARB BAY ZOOM**

Marlon Harwood

10 HE A LORD RAW MOON

ANSWERS ON PAGE 61

NEW SIGNINGS

There have been several new additions to the West Ham squad during the close season – here we look at the players who hope to make an impression in 2005/06

PAUL KONCHESKY:

Position: Defender/Midfielder
Date of Birth: 15/5/81
Birthplace: Barking
Height: 5ft 10ins
Former Clubs: Charlton Athletic, Tottenham
Career Record: 116 appearances + 68 sub, 6 goals
International Caps: 1 (England)

With approaching 200 appearances in the Premiership at Charlton and Spurs, Paul Konchesky brings with him knowledge and experience at the highest level. A former West Ham Academy youngster, he forged a successful career at The Valley and won his first England cap against Australia in February 2003 – a game played at Upton Park!

Konchesky, who made 15 appearances during a loan to Spurs, can play in defence or midfield and will provide excellent attacking options down the flank as well as keeping the opposition forwards at bay while doing his 'day job'!

Aged just 24, Konchesky will be hoping to use the move to the Hammers to re-launch his England career and prove that at just £1.5million, he is a bargain buy.

PETR MIKOLANDA:

Highly rated Czech striker Petr Mikolanda was handed a trial a few weeks before the start of the new season and certainly made the most of his opportunity. The 20-year-old Czech Republic Under-21 star then scored three goals in his first three appearances in pre-season and cannot wait to link up with his boyhood hero Teddy Sheringham during 2005/06. Mikolanda, an athletic, powerful forward, scored 13 goals for Viktoria Zizkov last season and he is hoping to continue his excellent progress in claret and blue.

"I am very happy to have signed at West Ham United," he said in August. "Teddy Sheringham was my hero when I was growing up. I remember watching his goal against Bayern Munich in the Champions League Final.

"I never dreamed that I would meet him, let alone be training alongside him. It's a fairytale."

DANNY GABBIDON:

Position: Central Defender
Date of Birth: 8/8/79
Birthplace: Cwmbran, Wales
Height: 5ft 10ins
Former Clubs: West Brom, Cardiff City
Career Record: 242 apps + 4 sub, 10 goals
International Caps: 17 (Wales)

Hardworking centre-half Danny Gabbidon began his career at West Brom, making 26 starts between 1998 and 2000. He then moved to Cardiff City, initially on loan for a month, then permanently for £175,000 in September 2000. It was while he was at Ninian Park that he really came to the fore, winning his first Welsh cap against the Czech Republic in March 2002. Since then, he's been a regular in the Welsh squad, earning a reputation as a hardworking defender with pace who can also man-mark with great effectiveness and will add a new dimension to a new-look defence this season.

JAMES COLLINS:

Position: Defender
Date of Birth: 23/8/83
Birthplace: Newport, Wales
Height: 6ft 2ins
Former Clubs: Cardiff City
Career Record: 62 apps + 24 sub, 6 goals
International Caps: 5 (Wales)

Signed on the same day as Cardiff City team-mate Danny Gabbidon, James Collins progressed through the youth system at Ninian Park and the 22-year-old defender is regarded as one of the brightest young Welsh talents around. He made his Bluebirds debut aged 17 and went to play well over 80 times for them during the five years was in the first team. He won the first of five Welsh caps against Norway in May 2004 and he looks set to become a regular fixture in the national side for many years to come. Though perhaps lacking in experience at the top level, Alan Pardew believes Collins will develop into a great player for West Ham over the coming years.

SHAKA HISLOP:

Position: Goalkeeper
Date of birth: 22/02/69
Birthplace: London
Height: 6ft 6ins
Weight: 12. 02
Previous clubs: Reading, Newcastle, West Ham, Portsmouth
Nationality: Trinidad & Tobago
Caps: N/A
Career Record: Pld: 431 Goals: 0

Shaka Hislop returned to Upton Park after signing on a free transfer shortly before the start of the 2005/06 season. Hislop played for the Hammers between 1998 and 2002, becoming a firm favourite with the fans before joining Portsmouth where he spent three years. A former Hammer of the Year in 1999, Hislop made 132 appearances during his first spell at Upton Park.

CLIVE CLARKE:

Position: Defender
Date of birth: 14/01/1980
Place of birth: Dublin
Height: 6ft 1ins
Weight: 12.03
Previous Clubs: Stoke City
Nationality: Ireland
Caps: 1
Career Record: Pld: 241 Sub: 21 Goals: 10

The 25-year-old Republic of Ireland international joined the Hammers from Stoke in July for a fee of £275,000. The Dublin-born left-back will be playing top-flight football for the first time having spent his entire career with Stoke. He began as a trainee in 1996, making his first team debut in 1999 and made 259 appearances for the Potteries side, scoring 10 goals.

SPOT THE BALL

A

1
3
2

ANSWERS ON

B

3
2
1

SPOT THE DIFFERENCE

Find 6 differences between these photos.

ANSWERS ON PAGE 61

NATURAL BORN LEADER
NIGEL REO-COKER

When Nigel Reo-Coker led West Ham out in the play-off final against Preston, it was the proudest moment of his young life. Having turned 21 on the day of the first leg semi final against Ipswich Town, the Hammers skipper – the youngest in the club's history – helped inspire his team-mates to the promised land of the Premiership with a typically tenacious, hard working and skilful performance against Preston.

A 21, he's likely to be the youngest captain in the top flight and throughout most of Europe, too, with many experts within the game predicting big things for the Southwark-born midfielder.

He began life at Wimbledon, signing from school for the homeless Dons and becoming a vital member of the first team after making his debut against Barnsley as a 17-year-old in April 2002. He became a regular in 2002/03 and was soon captaining the team, aged 19. He made 61 starts before joining the Hammers in January 2004 and made his debut in the 2-1 home win over Rotherham United. The England Under-19 regular soon became a firm favourite with West Ham fans, though his old club were eventually relegated.

He maintained a high level of consistency and is always encouraging his team-mates with his infectious, positive attitude. He was rewarded with a place in the England Under-20 team that played in the 2005 Toulon Tournament. Coach Peter Taylor singled Reo-Coker out for special praise and – surprise, surprise – made him captain!

Now the young star will be looking to make an impression on a higher stage with West Ham in the Premier League. He's certainly got the desire and ability to go all the way to the top.

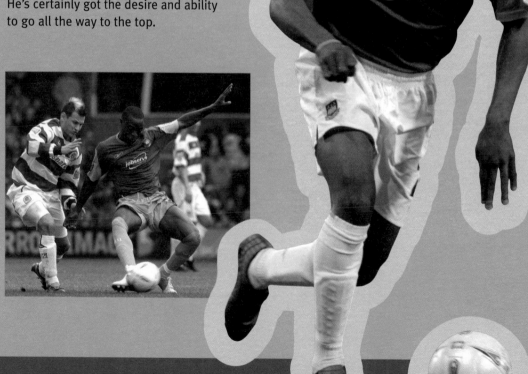

DREAM CATCHER

Mark Noble burst into the West Ham squad last season and he still can't believe how good it feels!

West Ham fans have always loved a local boy made good and Mark Noble is set to join a long list of illustrious names as he forges ahead on what looks set to be an exciting career. The England youth international has claret and blue blood running through his veins and his meteoric rise from the Under-18 squad at the start of the 2004/05 season to firm crowd favourite and first team squad regular is the stuff dreams are made of.

Every young Hammer dreams of playing for the club and for a lucky few, it actually happens. Mark Noble comes from a family of Hammers fans who still live close to the Boleyn Ground and have done for generations. The midfielder signed schoolboy forms aged 12 and during the summer of 2005, he signed a four-year contract with West Ham and capped an incredible year when he was voted Young Hammer of the Year and was runner-up to Teddy Sheringham in the senior award.

The Academy graduate made his debut in the FA Cup 3rd round tie with Norwich City. Manager Alan Pardew said: *"We think very highly of Mark. He and his family love this club and he's made a terrific start to his senior West Ham United career. If he keeps on working hard and continues to develop as he has, there is no reason why he cannot become a top player for this club."*

Mark made 10 starts last season and six more appearances from the bench and he also played in the play-off final win over Preston. An inspiration to any young supporter, Mark said he is still coming to terms with playing for the club he loves.

"All I ever wanted to do growing up was wear that West Ham United shirt," he said. *"I still can't believe that I'm playing for West Ham, it's like a dream that nobody can wake me up from. My Dad can't believe it either. He's been a West Ham fan since before I was born so imagine what it feels like for him to have his son playing at Upton Park. I look at him sometimes and expect him to give me a clip around the ear and tell me to wake up, because this really is a dream come true.*

"It's just incredible the feeling of running out at Upton Park, I just can't describe it. Some of the other lads look at me before a game and think I'm mad when I'm in the dressing room singing 'Bubbles' just before we're going to go up the tunnel. To hear the Upton Park crowd singing my name as well it's just fantastic. Last season was just brilliant, a dream come true!"

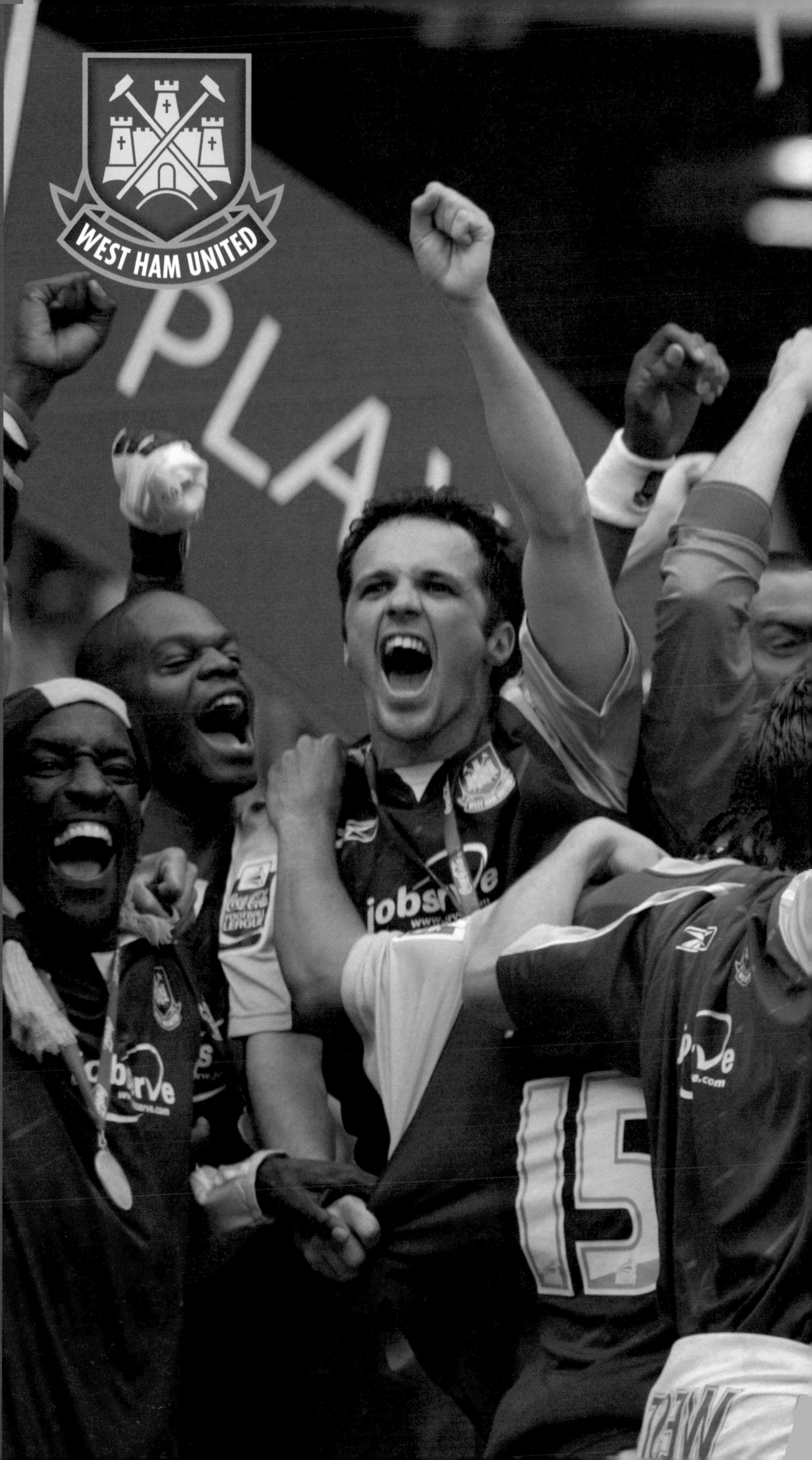
WEST HAM UNITED

WHO AM I?

ANSWERS ON PAGE 61

1 I began life at Dundee United and eventually moved to Derby County. I've also spent time at Blackburn Rovers – **who am I?**

2 I made my debut at Preston in 2004 and have come through the West Ham Academy. My brother plays for another Premiership team and is a former Hammer – **who am I?**

3 I was born in a place called Beer-Sheva and have played football for three clubs overseas. I play for my country but I'm not the first from my country to play for West Ham – **who am I?**

4 I broke into a Premiership side as a teenager and have spent time on loan at Royal Antwerp, Reading and Burnley before signing for the Hammers – **who am I?**

5 I began my career at Peterborough before moving to a Premiership team in 2000. I have three England Under-21 caps and was voted Player of the Year in 2003/04 – **who am I?**

6 I started out at the West Ham Academy but began league football with Bristol Rovers. I spent time with Bath City and had three successful years with a south coast club before moving to a Premiership team – **who am I?**

7 I signed for West Ham from a team in the Midlands and once scored for my old club at Upton Park in a FA Cup 3rd round tie – I cost the Hammers £500,000 – **who am I?**

8 I began my career with Hull City before moving to Wigan Athletic and have represented Northern Ireland many times at international level. I left another Premiership club to sign for the Hammers – **who am I?**

9 I have played football in Italy and was sent off on my West Ham debut. I recently signed a new deal at Upton Park – **who am I?**

10 I started out at Millwall and spent time on loan at Aldershot before joining Brian Clough's Nottingham Forest. A boyhood Hammers fan, I've also played for Spurs, Manchester United and Portsmouth – **who am I?**

10 FACTS ABOUT... MATTHEW ETHERINGTON

1 He was born in Truro, Cornwall on August 14, 1981

2 He first made his name at Peterborough United where he made his debut aged 15 and earned the nickname 'Mushy'

3 He signed for Spurs on New Year's Eve 1999 along with Simon Davies as part of a £1.2million deal

4 While at Spurs, he spent two months on loan at Bradford City, playing 13 times

5 He was once offered as part of a player plus cash deal by Spurs for Charlton's Scott Parker

6 He joined West Ham on August 4, 2003 from Spurs as part of a deal that saw Fredi Kanoute move in the opposite direction

7 He is a former England Under-21 international and made his debut against Slovenia, winning three caps in total

8 He made his Hammers debut against Preston North End, setting up both goals in a 2-1 win

9 He was voted Hammer of the Year for 2003/04

10 He once won £17,000 in a celebrity poker tournament

COME ON YOU IRONS!
THE HISTORY OF WEST HAM UNITED FC

West Ham United actually began life as the works team of ship building company Thames Ironworks in 1895 – hence the chant 'come on you Irons!' still heard at Upton Park today. In 1898 the club turned professional, joining the Southern League and playing their home games at Hermit Road – hopefully, that didn't reflect the attendances of the day!

In 1900, Thames Ironworks disbanded and reformed as West Ham United and in 1904 moved from their current home at the Memorial Grounds to the Boleyn Ground in Green Street, Upton Park, winning the first home game against Millwall 3-0 on September 2. It was a memorable day for Billy Bridgeman who bagged a hat-trick – not a bad start!

But it wasn't until 1919 that the Hammers were elected to the Football League and on August 30 of that year, Lincoln City were the first opponents in league football and the match ended 1-1. In a series of firsts around that time, Dutch side Haarlem were the first foreign side to play at Upton Park in a friendly and were left with a 4-2 defeat to remember their trip.

On April 28, 1923, West Ham competed in the first Wembley FA Cup final – later dubbed 'The White Horse' final because of the mounted police's attempts to keep an estimated crowd of 250,000 off the pitch! A white horse was among their number and, by all accounts, did sterling work on the day, though Bolton won

the game 2-0. The Hammers also became the first English team to visit Germany following the First World War and played their first First Division games that year, drawing 0-0 at Sunderland and beating Arsenal 1-0 at home that year.

There were no major events from that year until 1953, apart from relegation in 1932 and a seven-year break from league football from 1939-46 during the war. In '53 the Hammers played their first game under floodlights, beating Spurs 2-1 and two years later the first 'live' televised game took place as West Ham drew 0-0 with Holland Sports.

It was three years later before the first league game was played under floodlights and the Hammers again won, beating Bury 3-2. In 1958, the Hammers clinched the Division Two championship and later that year, on September 8, Bobby Moore made his first team debut at home to Manchester United. Ron Greenwood became manager in 1961 and would guide the club through an incredible era.

In 1964, many memorable historical games took place. The Hammers reached the League Cup semi-final, only to lose 6-3 on aggregate to Leicester but then defeated Preston 3-2 with the winner scored by Ronnie Boyce, to lift the FA Cup for the first time.

The great team of the Sixties returned to Wembley the following year to defeat TSV Munich 2-0 in the European Cup Winners' Cup final with Alan Sealey scoring both goals. In 1966 the Hammers lost the League Cup final (played over two legs) 5-3 on aggregate to West Brom. Meanwhile Hammers stars Geoff Hurst (3) and Martin Peters (1) scored all of England's goals between them in the 1966 World Cup final as England beat West Germany 4-2 in a team superbly captained by the legendary Bobby Moore – quite a feat!

In 1968 Geoff Hurst bagged six goals in the 8-0 defeat of Sunderland to equal Vic Watson's club record and two years later Martin Peters left for Spurs and Jimmy Greaves became a Hammer in a deal worth £200,000. John Lyall became assistant manager to Ron Greenwood in 1971 and a year later Martin Peters left for Stoke – two years after that, the club's greatest player, Bobby Moore, left for Fulham after 16 years as a first team regular. In one of the most memorable FA Cup finals of the era, West Ham met Fulham the following year at Wembley and Moore ended on the losing side in an emotional 2-0 defeat at Wembley. Alan Taylor scored both goals for the Hammers.

In 1976, Anderlecht triumphed 4-2 in the European Cup Winners' Cup final in Brussels and a year later, after a magnificent 16 years

as manager, Ron Greenwood left Upton Park to become England manager with John Lyall taking over as team boss for the Irons.

After relegation in 1978, West Ham returned to Wembley to beat Arsenal 1-0 in the 1980 FA Cup final with Trevor Brooking scoring a rare headed winner. A year later West Ham returned to Wembley to draw 1-1 with Liverpool in the League Cup but lost the replay 2-1. Promotion back to the top flight with a record number of points was achieved and in 1982 Billy Bonds passed Bobby Moore's appearance record when he made his 545th appearance for the club – he would go on to make more than 700 appearances in total.

In 1986 the Hammers finished third in the First Division behind champions Liverpool and runners-up Everton for what is still our highest ever league finish. Just three years later and John Lyall was sacked after 34 years service following relegation from the top flight. In February 24 1993, Bobby Moore, the club's greatest player, died of bowel cancer aged 51 and Upton Park became a shrine to this amazing player and wonderful man.

A few months later and the club clinched promotion to the Premiership for the first time and less than a year after his death, the new South Stand lower tier was opened and named The Bobby Moore Stand.

In 1999 the Hammers finish fifth in the league and later lift the Intertoto Cup with a 3-2 aggregate win over Metz to secure UEFA Cup football for the first time. A year later young Academy graduate Rio Ferdinand becomes the world's costliest defender as he signs for Leeds for £18million – Joe Cole and Frank Lampard a few years later also leave in big money deals.

In May 2004, after a two-year absence, West Ham return to the Premiership with a victory over Preston North End under the management of Alan Pardew. It's good to be back!

SILHOUETTES

Can you guess the identity of two of our team?

ANSWERS ON PAGE 61

42

HAMMERS CROSSWORD

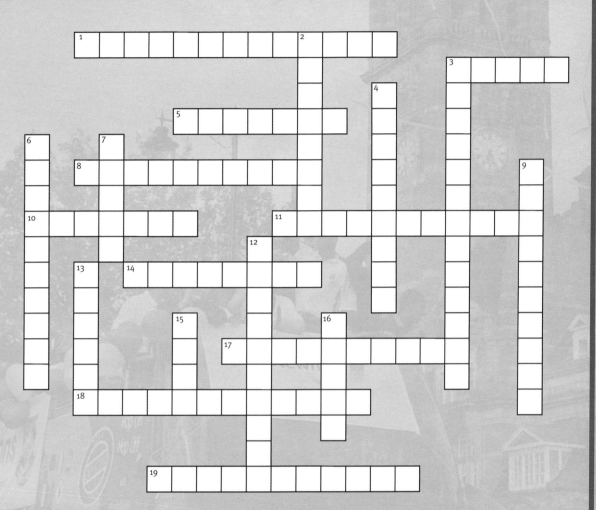

ACROSS:

1 England Under-18 star who signed from Millwall

3 Chris, the Academy star who has played for the first team

5 Team Jimmy Walker joined from

8 All-time Hammers legend who won 108 England caps

10 Team former favourites Joe and Frank left for West Ham

11 The man with all the kit

14 Carl, who used to play with Bournemouth

17 First team coach

18 Anton's England international relative

19 Signed last season on loan from MSK Zilina

DOWN:

2 England Under-18 prospect

3 The Hammers' training HQ

4 Former name of club Nigel-Reo Coker signed from

6 Northern Ireland international who signed during last summer

7 Mark, the Young Player of the Year for 2005

9 Hard man who signed a new deal in the summer

12 Which works team did the Hammers begin life as in 1895?

13 Former boss glenn, now at Newcastle United

15 Use the force! First name of former Man United winger

16 First name of young Aussie defender who was on loan at MK Dons

43

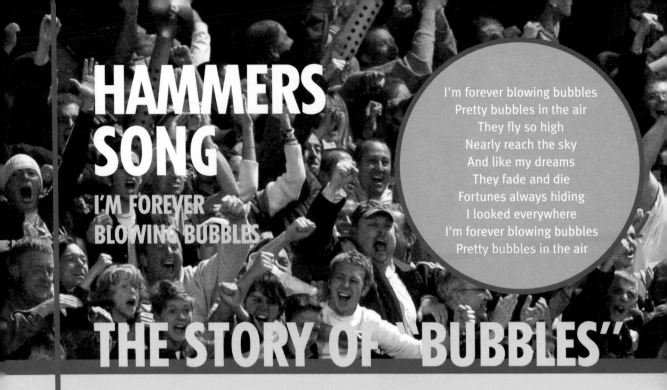

HAMMERS SONG

I'M FOREVER BLOWING BUBBLES

I'm forever blowing bubbles
Pretty bubbles in the air
They fly so high
Nearly reach the sky
And like my dreams
They fade and die
Fortunes always hiding
I looked everywhere
I'm forever blowing bubbles
Pretty bubbles in the air

THE STORY OF "BUBBLES"

I'm Forever Blowing Bubbles was written by American composer James Brockman in the early 1920s and became a hit on both sides of the Atlantic.

But it was not until around 1926 that the tune was first sung at Upton Park.

At that time schoolboy soccer was extremely popular and there were often more than 1000 spectators around the touchlines of pitches in the West Ham area for matches between teams of 14-year-olds.

The West Ham Schools League was divided into sections, with championship matches at the end of the season between the Elementary schools.

One of the West Ham champions was Park School, situated near West Ham Park in the Upton area and its headmaster was Cornelius Beal, who had a penchant for music and rhymes.

He wrote special words to the tune of "Bubbles" and when any Park School player was having a good game, spectators mentioned him by name in the ditty.

In those days District schoolboys' teams often played at the Boleyn Ground so it naturally followed that "Corney" Beal's version of the song should be heard during matches on the Hammers' pitch.

Although the association of "Bubbles" with schools' football faded away, the song lingered in the minds of Hammers fans.

The late Mr P Crumpler, of Leigh-on-Sea, Essex, who worked at Beckton Gas Works, recalled that the Company Band "were engaged by the West Ham

United Football Club to play for 20 minutes before the kick-off and for ten minutes at the interval."

He added: "We played 'Bubbles' and it very quickly became a favourite with the crowd. If we didn't play 'Bubbles' the crowd would sing it anyway."

In later years the tradition was carried on by the "K" Division Metropolitan Police Band and the Leyton Silver Band.

The tradition was firmly established before World War II and the song was heard at Wembley in June 1940, when the Hammers played in the Football League War Cup Final against Blackburn Rovers.

It reached the peak of the Wembley "hit parade" in 1964 when the club played Preston North End in the FA Cup Final – even though the official music arranger and community singing organiser tried to substitute "Maybe It's Because I'm a Londoner."

Hammers fans quickly scotched that idea by drowning out the Guards Band!

The Hammers' entry into European competition in 1965 took the song to the Continent with the team and it was back again at Wembley for the European Cup Winners' Cup Final in 1965.

Today, the song is heard not only at soccer matches but also at social functions attended by Hammers fans.

Many Continentals are also so well aware of the connection that there is never any difficulty in getting them to join in when Hammers' teams play abroad.

The Hammers can truly claim to be the first soccer club to have their own "top of the pops."

THE CLUB BADGE

The two main features of the West Ham United crest are a pair of crossed hammers and a castle.

The hammers are often believed to derive from the fact that the Club was formed in West Ham, while its present ground was actually over the Borough border in what was formerly East Ham. This is not correct, as the crossed hammers were a motif in use before the formation of West Ham United.

When the Thames Ironworks club was formed in 1895 the hammers were adopted as the badge, being symbolic of tools used in shipbuilding. This is the derivation of the nickname "Hammers", although the team was also known as "The Irons"; hence there is still heard from the terrace: "Come on you Irons!"

The castle was traditionally believed to be connected with Henry VIII's second Queen, Anne Boleyn. However, this was not founded on fact, as the "castle" was indeed a building known as Green Street House.

The House was built in 1544, eight years after the execution of Anne Boleyn. A couple of turrets were added two years later "to enhance the beauty of the grounds", and one remained on the Green Street frontage until well after World War II.

For some years a drawing of this turret featured on the cover of the club programme, and when the present badge was designed and first used in 1968 this feature was incorporated.

The buildings had many subsequent uses. In turn it had been a reformatory, a Priory for an order associated with the Catholic Church, the Boleyn Club (with a bowling green at the rear), and offices for West Ham United F.C. when bomb-damage necessitated evacuation from the area in the West Stand during World War II. The whole structure is now demolished, and a school is on the original site.

Connections with those early days are now permanently fixed by other names in the vicinity: Castle Street and Priory Road are on two sides of the ground.

Several roads in the area are named after Henry VIII's six wives, among them being Boleyn Road; there is also a Boleyn Tavern.

The Club has a copyright on the design.

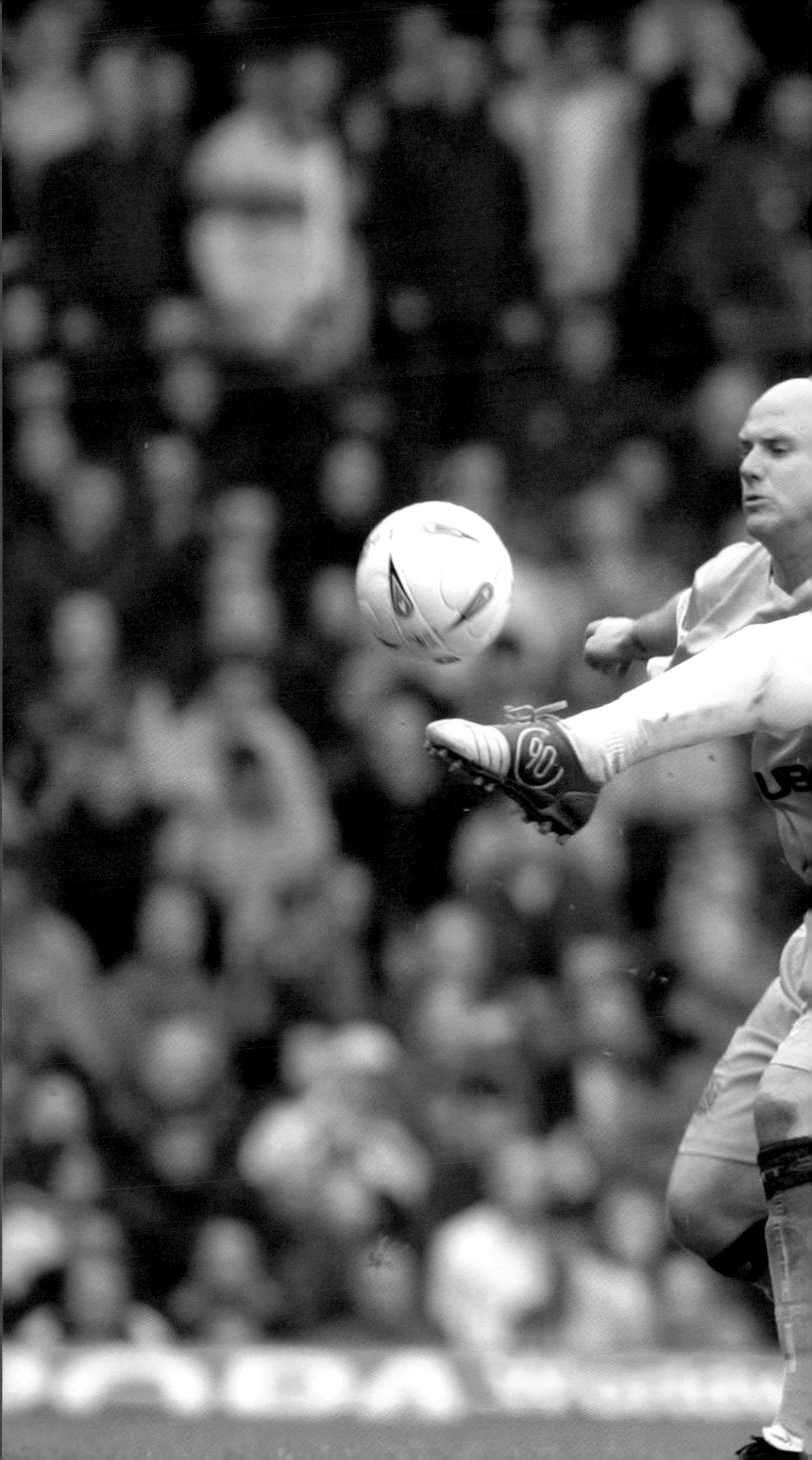

PLAYER PROFILES

STEPHEN BYWATER
Came on as substitute in the play-off final win over Preston. Bywater is a promising young goalkeeper who is still only 24 and made his debut in the Premiership aged 18. Signed from Rochdale, the Manchester-born shot-stopper has spent time on loan at Wycombe and Hull City and will be looking to challenge Jimmy Walker and Roy Carroll for the No.1 spot this season.

He is still registered with West Ham but temporarily on loan to another club.

ROY CARROLL
Northern Ireland international Roy Carroll became one of the first signings of the close season when he arrived from Manchester United, where he won Premiership and FA Cup winners' medals after spending four years at Old Trafford. He has also played for Hull City and Wigan Athletic.

JIMMY WALKER
Jimmy Walker joined West Ham in June 2004 on a free transfer from Walsall for whom he made more than 400 appearances. Played 17 times during his first season with the Hammers and suffered a nasty knee injury in the play-off final win over Preston.

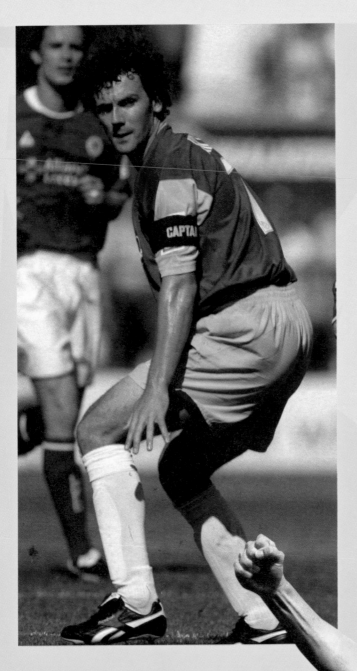

CHRISTIAN DAILLY

Scottish international Christian Dailly will begin his fourth season as a Hammer this year and will use his Premiership experience to help the younger defenders in the squad make the adjustments to life in the Premiership. A defender of immense experience for club and country.

JAMES COLLINS

Welsh international James Collins arrived from Cardiff City as part of a double deal with Danny Gabbidon. The 22-year-old centre back made his debut for Cardiff aged 17 and made 86 appearances for the Bluebirds before moving to the Hammers last July.

TOMAS REPKA

The Czech international committed himself to the Hammers during the close season and Repka's experience will prove crucial to the team as they re-adjust to life in the Premiership. He joined from Italian side Fiorentina for a Club record of £5million in September 2001 and is now one of the longest serving players at Upton Park.

PAUL KONCHESKY

England international Paul Konchesky made the Hammers his third London club when he joined from Charlton Athletic, having also played for Tottenham. Comfortable as full-back or in midfield, he actually began his career with the Hammers as a youth player and returns to the Boleyn Ground with a wealth of Premiership experience.

DANNY GABBIDON

Danny Gabbidon is an experienced Welsh international who has played many times for Wales since making his debut in 2002 against Tomas Repka's Czech Republic. Quick and tenacious, he notched up more than 200 appearances for his former club Cardiff and will be a tremendous asset to Alan Pardew's side.

TRENT MCCLENAHAN

Led Australia in the FIFA World Youth Championships last summer and looks to be a fine prospect. The young defender was loaned to MK Dons last season to gain vital experience of league football and will be hoping to make more first team appearances during 2005/06.

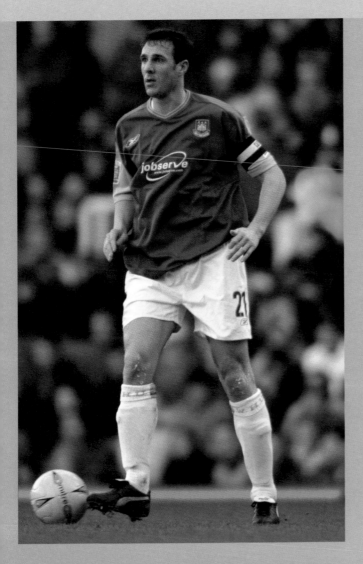

MALKY MACKAY

Signed from Norwich for £300,000, Malky is a no-nonsense defender who joined the Hammers in September 2004. Injury restricted his first team appearances during his first season at Upton Park but the former Celtic star and Scotland international will be hoping for better things this year.

ELLIOTT WARD

A young defender who has graduated through the West Ham Academy to the first team, though the centre-back spent much of last season out as he recovered from a back operation. He signed a new deal for the club last summer and broke into the team towards the end of last season with a series of commanding displays alongside Ferdinand including the play-off final win over Preston.

ANTON FERDINAND

Anton has followed in his brother Rio's footsteps by progressing through the Academy to establish himself in the first team as a teenager. The young defender has grown in stature the more games he has played and is already among the most coveted talents in the country.

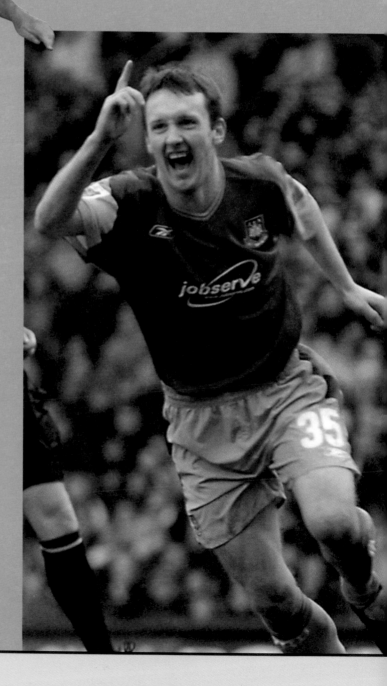

CHRIS COHEN

Versatility is the main asset of Academy starlet Chris Cohen. He can play pretty much anywhere along the back line and across midfield. The 19 year-old made 18 appearances in his first two seasons in the senior squad and skippered the reserves last year.

GAVIN WILLIAMS

Welsh star Gavin Williams signed from Yeovil Town last season at a cost of £250,000, shortly before the end of 2004. The former Hereford United midfielder was bought to add competition to the wide attacking areas of the team. He has many tricks in his locker and is set to become a firm crowd favourite in future seasons.

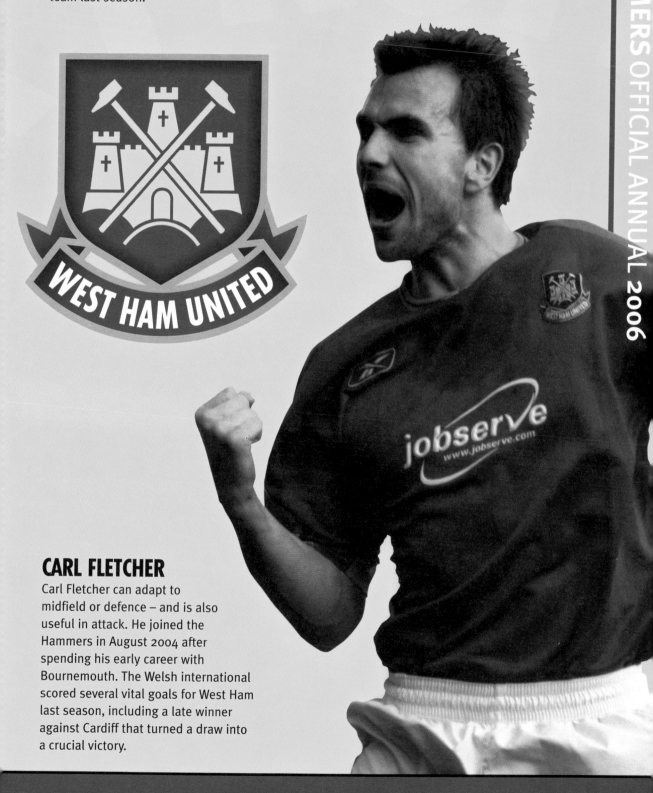

MOSES ASHIKODI

An explosive Academy striker tipped to appear on the first team fringes this season, Moses Ashikodi has already represented England at Under-18 level and was a star of the Hammers' youth team last season.

CARL FLETCHER

Carl Fletcher can adapt to midfield or defence – and is also useful in attack. He joined the Hammers in August 2004 after spending his early career with Bournemouth. The Welsh international scored several vital goals for West Ham last season, including a late winner against Cardiff that turned a draw into a crucial victory.

MATTHEW ETHERINGTON

An attacking midfielder who joined from Spurs, Matty Etherington was an instant hit during his first year at Upton Park, winning the Hammer of the Year in 2004. The England Under-21 international was influential during last season, though often the subject of one or two man-markers for many of the games. He will be once again looking forward to showing what he can do at Premiership level this season.

HAYDEN MULLINS

Hayden became Alan Pardew's first signing for West Ham when he joined, initially on loan, from Crystal Palace, last season. A wonderful athlete, the versatile midfielder is also comfortable in defence and played a vital role in promotion last season. He bagged two Player of the Year awards at Palace and is an exciting addition to Pardew's squad.

NIGEL REO-COKER

A natural leader, Nigel Reo-Coker was only too happy to take on the captain's armband when asked last season. He joined in January 2004 and soon became an instant hit with the Hammers' faithful after signing from Wimbledon where he was one of the youngest captain's ever in the First Division. He has represented England at most levels and is tipped for full international honours with his country in the not-too-distant future.

SHAUN NEWTON

Signed initially on loan as cover for Tomas Repka, Shaun Newton filled the right-back role admirably, becoming a popular figure towards the end of last season. The 30-year-old has enjoyed spells with Charlton Athletic and Wolves during his career.

LUKE CHADWICK

Luke will be hoping to re-ignite his Premiership career with the Hammers this season after bursting on the scene as a talented teenager with Manchester United during 2000/01. Tipped for big things, injury then struck and he found it hard to win back his place in the starting line-up and instead joined Reading and then Burnley on loan. He signed for Pardew for the second time when he joined at the start of last season and was a vital attacking outlet, claiming many assists, mainly from his right-wing berth.

He is still registered with West Ham but temporarily on loan to another club.

HOGAN EPHRAIM

Yet another Academy starlet who is tagged to have a bright future, Hogan Ephraim made a real impact for England Under-17s when he bagged four goals against Russia. An attacking midfielder, the Islington-born youngster is definitely one for the future and a player we will be soon hearing lots more of.

BOBBY ZAMORA

A West Ham fan as a boy, former Brighton striker Bobby Zamora couldn't have timed his return to form last season any better. His goals in the play-off semi-final against Ipswich came at critical stages and his sublime second strike at Portman Road would win any goal of the season awards at any club. Who better, then, to score the winning goal that sent the Hammers back to the Premiership? After all, it's Zamora....

TEDDY SHERINGHAM

Teddy will celebrate his 40th birthday during this season and will likely be one – if not the – oldest players in the Premiership. But he proved age is nothing more than numbers last year with his experience the vital factor in West Ham's return to the top division. His predatory instincts and link-up play were invaluable to Pardew's largely youthful team and he will again be a crucial member of the first team squad for 2005/06.

MARLON HAREWOOD

The former Nottingham Forest striker is an explosive talent who can unnerve defenders with his pace and strength and has benefited from having the experience of Teddy Sheringham to learn off in the past year. Signed for just £500,000, Marlon played in all but one of The Championship games, notching up 21 goals in all competitions. He was watched by a number of Premiership sides last season but committed himself to Upton Park by signing a new four-year deal during the close season.

MARK NOBLE

One of several first team regulars to have come through the Academy system at West Ham, Mark Noble became an instant hit with the fans when he broke into the team midway through last season. Such was the-then 17-year-old's impact that he was voted runner-up to Teddy Sheringham in the Hammer of the Year award 2005 and also picked up the Young Hammer of the Year award for good measure. Tipped to be a real star of the future, the sky is the limit for the former England Under-16 skipper.

YOSSI BENAYOUN

Israeli international Yossi Benayoun signed from Spanish club Racing Santander during the close season for £2.5m. The 25-year-old midfielder was top scorer for the Spaniards last season and the creative playmaker was advised to sign by fellow Israeli and former West Ham favourite Eyal Berkovic. Like Eyal, Yossi has the ability to unlock defences with perfectly weighted through balls and is likely to be a huge hit with the Upton Park faithful.

MARLON HAREWOO

TOMAS REPKA

CLUB HONOURS

DOMESTIC

Football League: Division One Best position: 3rd 1985-86
Division Two Champions: 1957-58, 1980-81
Runners-Up: 1922-23; 1990-91; 1992-93

FA CUP

Winners: 1964, 1975, 1980
Runners-up: 1923

FOOTBALL LEAGUE CUP

Runners-up: 1966, 1981

FA CHARITY SHIELD

Winners: 1964-65 (shared)

EUROPEAN COMPETITION

European Cup Winners' Cup: Winners: 1964-65
Runners-Up: 1975-76

UEFA INTERTOTO CUP

Winners: 1999

YOUTH

FA Youth Cup: Winners: 1963, 1981, 1999
Runners-up: 1957, 1959, 1975, 1996
South-East Counties Champions: 1984-85, 1995-96, 1997-98
FA Premier Youth Academy Under-19 Champions: 1998-99, 1999-2000

ANSWERS PAGE

P15 SEASON QUIZ

1. Teddy Sheringham scored and Luke Chadwick crossed the ball
2. Chris Cohen and the final scores was 1-0 to West Ham
3. Callum Davenport, Chris Powell and Carl Fletcher – Chris Powell was an unused sub
4. Matthew Etherington
5. Teddy Sheringham and Bobby Zamora
6. Mauricio Taricco – after sustaining injury a week into his new deal at West Ham, he offered to terminate his contract to save the club money and find a new player.
7. Ipswich 2-0 – the goals came in the first and last minutes of the game
8. Andy Melville
9. James Tomkins
10. Bobby Zamora

P22 WORDSEARCH

1. Stuart Pearce
2. Boleyn Ground
3. Preston
4. Blackburn
5. Bubbles
6. Wolves
7. Marlon Harewood
8. Claret
9. Irons
10. Brooking

P23 NAME GAME

1. BROKEN LAM = Mark Noble
2. STAMP ARE OK = Tomas Repka
3. MADE SHY NUN ILL = Hayden Mullins
4. WHALED KICK U C = Luke Chadwick
5. DONNER NAAN RIFT = Anton Ferdinand
6. IS HANG DRY THEMED = Teddy Sheringham
7. ROCK LINE GEORGE = Nigel Reo Coker
8. LO CAR LORRY = Roy Carroll
9. BARB BAY ZOOM = Bobby Zamora
10. HE A LORD RAW MOON = Marlon Harewood

P28 SPOT THE BALL

A 2
B 1

P29 SPOT THE DIFFERENCE

1. Chord on waistband missing
   Yellow Reebok logo
   No stripe on collar
2. Stripe on right hand sleeve
   Dot on Jobserve logo missing
   Number one missing from shorts

P42 SILHOUETTES

1. Carl Fletcher
2. Marlon Harewood

P36 WHO AM I?

1. Christian Dailly
2. Anton Ferdinand
3. Yossi Benayoun
4. Luke Chadwick
5. Matthew Etherington
6. Bobby Zamora
7. Marlon Harewood
8. Roy Carroll
9. Tomas Repka
10. Teddy Sheringham

P43 CROSSWORD

Across

1. Moses Ashikodi
3. Cohen
5. Walsall
8. Bobby Moore
10. Chelsea
11. Eddie Gillam
14. Fletcher
17. Peter Grant
18. Rio Ferdinand
19. Dusan Kuciak

Down

2. Kyel Reid
3. Chadwell Heath
4. Wimbledon
6. Roy Carroll
7. Noble
9. Tomas Repka
12. Thames Iron
13. Roeder
15. Luke
16. Trent

COCA-COLA CHAMPIONSHIP PLAY OF

WEST HAM UNITED